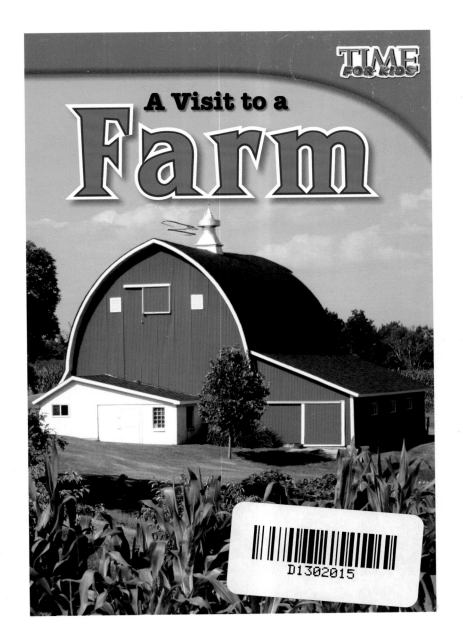

A Visit to a
Farm

TIME
FOR KIDS

D. M. Rice

Consultant

Timothy Rasinski, Ph.D.
Kent State University

Publishing Credits

Dona Herweck Rice, *Editor-in-Chief*
Robin Erickson, *Production Director*
Lee Aucoin, *Creative Director*
Conni Medina, M.A.Ed., *Editorial Director*
Jamey Acosta, *Editor*
Stephanie Reid, *Photo Editor*
Rachelle Cracchiolo, M.S.Ed., *Publisher*

Based on writing from *TIME For Kids*.

Teacher Created Materials

5301 Oceanus Drive
Huntington Beach, CA 92649-1030
http://www.tcmpub.com

ISBN 978-1-4333-3608-9

© 2012 by Teacher Created Materials, Inc..

BP 5028

Table of Contents

Going to the Farm

Last summer, my brother and I visited my grandparents' farm. Our dad drove us there.

He gave me a camera so I could make a book about our visit.

Grandma and Grandpa were there to meet us, along with their dog, Buddy.

They were all happy to see us.

After our dad left, Grandma asked us, "What would you like to see?" We said, "Everything!"

So Grandma, Grandpa, and Buddy showed us the farm.

The Barn and Silos

First, we saw the big, red
barn. The barn is big so
that the animals and farm
machines can fit inside.

Grandpa said that he milks the cows in the barn and keeps his **tractor** there, too.

Next to the barn are tall **silos**.

The silos store the grain from the farm. The grain feeds the animals in the winter.

Next, we saw the horse **corral**. There were horses and ponies standing nose to nose. They looked like they were talking to each other.

One horse was near the fence.

Grandpa gave my brother a carrot to feed the horse. He ate that carrot right out of my brother's hand!

Beyond the corral, we
saw the cows in the **pasture**.
Some were eating and some
were just standing or lying
down.

One small calf was getting
milk from its mother.

The Fields

When we left the pasture, I heard a low roar. I asked Grandpa, "What is that noise?" He said, "It is one of the farm machines. Come and see."

Grandpa and Grandma
took us to the wheat fields.

A man was driving a large machine.

Grandpa said that it was a **combine** used to harvest the grain.

We waved to the man. He waved back. Then Buddy barked and wagged his tail. He was waving, too!

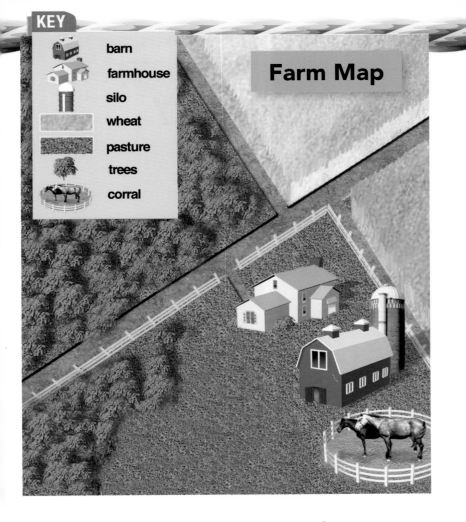

barn

farmhouse

silo

wheat

pasture

trees

corral

Farm Map

Our grandparents' farm
is big. Here is a map of the
farm. Maybe one day you can
visit, too.

Glossary

barn

combine

corral

pasture

silos

tractor